One-Minute Prayers™

FOR MY *Daughter*

Text by *Hope Lyda*

HARVEST HOUSE PUBLISHERS

EUGENE, OREGON

Cover by Garborg Design Works, Minneapolis, Minnesota

Cover photo © Kevin Russ/iStockphoto.com

ONE-MINUTE PRAYERS is a series trademark of The Hawkins Children's LLC. Harvest House Publishers, Inc., is the exclusive licensee of the trademark ONE-MINUTE PRAYERS.

ONE-MINUTE PRAYERS™ FOR MY DAUGHTER
Copyright © 2006 by Harvest House Publishers
Published by Harvest House Publishers
Eugene, Oregon 97402
www.harvesthousepublishers.com

ISBN-13: 978-0-7369-1864-0
ISBN-10: 0-7369-1864-7

Printed in the United States of America

06 07 08 09 10 11 12 13 14 / BP-MS / 10 9 8 7 6 5 4 3 2 1

Contents

Listen, O daughter, consider and give ear...
The king is enthralled by your beauty; honor
him, for he is your lord.

PSALM 45:10

Radiant

*Your beauty should not come from outward adorn-
ment, such as braided hair and the wearing of
gold jewelry and fine clothes. Instead, it should be
that of your inner self, the unfading beauty of a
gentle and quiet spirit, which is of great worth in
God's sight.*

1 PETER 3:3-5

Without any adornment or earthly additions, my
daughter came into this world beautiful and unspoiled.
I knew she was complete as she was the moment I saw
her. I desired to protect her from anything that might
change her, hurt her, or take her from me.

Now I see how life needs to happen—with all its
messiness and splendor. All experiences will shape this
child I hold so dear. Her beauty will not be lessened
but will become more radiant as she blossoms in the
care of Your perfecting love.

Wonder

All My Praise

Give thanks to the LORD, call on his name;
make known among the nations what he has done.
Sing to him, sing praise to him;
tell of all his wonderful acts.

1 CHRONICLES 16:8-9

I want to tell the world about the love I feel for my child. I know this love comes from You, this daughter comes as a gift from You. Your goodness has always carried me, but this deep joy I have as a parent surpasses all other wonders.

My lips will praise You daily. Even when I am tired, frustrated, and dealing with the hard work of being a parent, I will turn my face to Yours and show my daughter who leads us, who cares for us, and who loves us unconditionally. I will teach her Your name.

May She Know

I praise you because I am fearfully and wonder-
fully made;
your works are wonderful,
I know that full well.

PSALM 139:14

Hold my daughter's heart in Your hand, Lord. Wipe away her tears when I am not there to do so. Reach for her hand when I am miles away. And when she is too old for me to pick up, lift her up so that she can see the wonders of this life set out before her.

My job is to direct her in Your ways, Your knowledge, Your truth. I pray for each of her steps, that they will be aligned with Your will for her. Most of all, I pray that she will know You fully, personally—and that she will praise You all of her days.

Power

Therefore once more I will astound these people with wonder upon wonder.

ISAIAH 29:14

The wonders You bestow upon us show Your power and strength, Lord. Underneath the innocence and beauty of my daughter's life is a current of such wonder. It is a mighty force that grows within her heart and soul. You have shaped her, and You have placed the seed of possibility in her.

I see Your loving touch in the shape of her ears, her face, her toes. As much as the miracle of her life astounds me, I am equally moved by the power of the miracles in her life yet unseen. I watch with amazement to see what comes next.

A Personal Prayer for My Daughter

Love

Just Like Me

*The LORD is slow to anger, abounding in love and
forgiving sin and rebellion.*

NUMBERS 14:18

I felt the heat of anger rise up in me today as I
watched my daughter do something with defiance. I
had to take a few minutes to calm down and clear my
head. The hardest part about seeing that look on my
daughter's face is that I know it from my own reflec-
tion. How many times have I tested Your patience,
Your love?

My heart softens when I recognize Your abounding
love reaching out to me time after time. May I be an
example of this grace to my daughter so that when she
is in need of forgiveness, she will seek Your open arms
just as I have done so many times before.

Sweetness

A new command I give you: Love one another.
As I have loved you, so you must love one another.

JOHN 13:34

My daughter's teacher passed out treats at school today. Quickly the children fell in line to receive their prize for a job well done. The lead child passed the treat to the next and so on until they all had one. They all knew they would receive a treat, so they easily released the box of cupcakes to the next child in line without worry or envy.

If my daughter knows Your love is more than enough for her life, she will be willing and eager to pass along love to those she encounters. You have plenty for everyone. Lord, give my daughter a heart that overflows with the sweetness of Your love. And give her the desire and patience to pass it on.

Thirst

Many waters cannot quench love;
rivers cannot wash it away.

SONG OF SOLOMON 8:7

Can I protect my daughter from heartbreak? I would move mountains to save her from such hurt. I worry that a boy or a friend will cast her away. She will grow from it. She might change. I pray she gains wisdom.

Lord, Your endless source of love is the only thing that will quench her thirst for acceptance and worth. No man or friend will do that for her. Nobody, not even I, can offer the unconditional and unrelenting love that pours from Your heart toward her spirit. Give her a thirst that draws her to the river of Your mercy and grace. And may her thirst be satisfied with the living water.

A Personal Prayer for My Daughter

Health

Comfort

I will heal my people and will let them enjoy abundant peace and security.

JEREMIAH 33:6

I enjoy bringing comfort to my daughter when she is scared or hurt. When I hold her close and wipe away tears, peace overcomes her worry, and security replaces her fear. Lord, how much more do You comfort her. Your Spirit of peace will cover her when she faces trials much bigger than a scraped knee or a fear of the night.

Each time You hold us close, Your peace eases all of our anxieties. You calm the storm within us, and we rest in the security of Your protective arms.

Smile

A cheerful look brings joy to the heart,
and good news gives health to the bones.

PROVERBS 15:30

Her smile brightens my day. With just a glance, my daughter can melt my heart and turn a rough day into a promising one. In the busyness of life, when I check my watch and my to-do list countless times, remind me to offer her a cheerful look, a smile, a wink. Allow my actions to bring her peace and assurance.

The security I have in You is a gift I can pass along to her. When my nature wants to lean toward negative emotions, help me trust Your plan, Your schedule for my day. Direct my actions so that I bring joy to my daughter's heart and health to her spirit.

The Answer

*O LORD my God, I called to you for help
and you healed me.*

PSALM 30:2

I try to explain to my child how Your ways are mysterious, difficult to define and place in a box marked "God." This is hard for her to grasp. The unknowns, the questions that enter my adult mind and lead me to deeper understanding, only cause her to stumble.

Lord, may the healing answer I offer my daughter be one of simplicity. All she needs to know is that when she prays, when she calls to You, You hear her little voice and answer her. The only thing she needs to know is that You call her "daughter."

A Personal Prayer
for My Daughter

Friendship

What We Wear

Therefore, as God's chosen people, holy and dearly loved, clothe yourselves with compassion, kindness, humility, gentleness and patience.

COLOSSIANS 3:12

I stood in the doorway to my daughter's room for most of the morning as she decided what to wear to school. My patience was spent after several minutes, and my tolerance dwindled. How did her appearance become so much more important than other factors like timeliness and obedience?

Do we spend a fraction of that time determining what we will wear spiritually each day? Grant me the wisdom to teach my daughter how to adorn her spirit in order to be a better friend and a more fulfilled person. May she stand in front of the mirror of Your eyes clothed in compassion, kindness, humility, gentleness, and patience.

Choosing Sides

*Anyone who chooses to be a friend of the world
becomes an enemy of God.*

JAMES 4:4

I already see how my daughter's loyalties are torn in different directions. She is making friends and discovering that the way these friends see her and treat her affects her emotions and feelings of worth. Give her eyes to see how her friendship also impacts others. May she not become so dedicated to status or popularity that she sacrifices the gifts of relationship, serving, and community.

Help me encourage my daughter to choose You and her identity in You over the offerings of society and culture. Lead her to share her heart for You with those she calls "friend."

Honor

*Be devoted to one another in brotherly love. Honor
one another above yourselves.*

ROMANS 12:10

"Honor" seems like a word from yesteryear, when
knights and damsels in distress engaged in or inspired
battle for the sake of honor. Encourage us to bring
honor back into the language of today. Help us recognize honorable actions and words with praise and
appreciation. Remind us to shun that which is dishon-
orable to You and Your children.

Restore a sense of honor in my daughter's friend-
ships. Teach her to respect relationships by infusing
them with truth, integrity, and faithfulness. Give her a
heart to become a servant in Your kingdom so that she
honors You with her life.

A Personal Prayer
for My Daughter

Future

Blessings to Come

*Your beginnings will seem humble,
so prosperous will your future be.*

JOB 8:7

What will my daughter become? Where will she live as an adult? How will she carry herself and share her faith? Lord, I know that You want great things for her. Your vision of her days is clearer than my clouded expectations. I pray her future will be filled with such blessings—the riches of friends, family, and purpose.

I cannot know for certain whom my daughter will become. But I know her today, and I see the gift of Your future in her eyes.

Beyond the Trials

There is surely a future hope for you,
and your hope will not be cut off.

PROVERBS 23:18

∽

Childhood comes with its share of disappointments. My daughter is eager to grow up, show her independence, and make her own mistakes. I explain how today's stumbling blocks become stepping-stones for tomorrow's purpose.

Lord, grant my daughter contentment for today and wisdom to get through the trials big and small—all the while creating in her a heart that believes in the future hope You have for her.

On Today's Plate

Therefore do not worry about tomorrow,
for tomorrow will worry about itself.
Each day has enough trouble of its own.

MATTHEW 6:34

What is in store for us today, Lord? More adventures of love, living, and giving? I want to view each day as an opportunity for me to teach my daughter about You and Your will. Help me show her the portion of life on her plate today so she does not worry about tomorrow.

Lord, I don't want to miss a moment with my daughter as she discovers all that You have for her. Slow us down. Direct our attention to what is important in Your eyes. May our attention not wander beyond what is immediately before us, and help us face tomorrow fresh and not weary, blessed and not defeated.

A Personal Prayer
for My Daughter

Wisdom

Out of the Mouth of Babes

She speaks with wisdom,
and faithful instruction is on her tongue.

PROVERBS 31:26

You have taught me so much through my daughter. She speaks wisdom into my life on a daily basis. I pray for her continued growth as a wise, godly woman. I know she will face many exciting and difficult transitions as she matures. Give her the courage to cling to her knowledge of You and Your way.

When I want to be the parent and speak on my daughter's behalf, remind me that You formed her by Your hands as an individual with a very unique identity in You. Remind me to slow down and listen to what she has to say, and help me hold my tongue long enough to hear the wisdom that comes from Your child's lips.

Wholeheartedly

Teach me your way, O Lord,
and I will walk in your truth;
give me an undivided heart,
that I may fear your name.

PSALM 86:11

My daughter is passionate about her pursuits. She takes on a task of interest and pours her heart and soul into it. I love how You have made her this way. What passions will be a part of her future, I wonder? What will You give her to spark her imagination, energy, and diligence?

Creator, I pray my daughter will always have a heart that hungers for You and Your wisdom. What a wonderful life she will enjoy if she seeks Your truth wholeheartedly. Protect the passion of this young girl— may it serve You in the days and years to come.

I Want

Flee the evil desires of youth, and pursue righteousness, faith, love and peace, along with those who call on the Lord out of a pure heart.

2 TIMOTHY 2:22

The arm unfurls, the hand extends, and the finger points. I know these motions of my daughter's limbs because they are constant impulses for her. Try as I might, I cannot seem to dissuade her from wanting things that are beyond her reach, beyond her needs, beyond Your will for her.

Give my daughter eyes that catch the shimmer and attraction of those qualities and pursuits that are of You. Give her a heart that wants to be wise and pure in the ways of faith, love, and peace. Let her "I wants" become pleasing acts of obedience.

A Personal Prayer
for My Daughter

Self

Privilege

All the days ordained for me
were written in your book
before one of them came to be.

PSALM 139:16

Perhaps the greatest gift I can give my daughter is a sense of belonging to You. She doesn't need to think like me, act like her friends, or follow a path we expect of her. She does, however, have the privilege of becoming what You have ordained for her journey.

In what ways can I become a better example of this kind of living, Lord? Help me free myself and my daughter from the restrictions we place upon ourselves so that we might truly discover what each page in the book of life holds for us as individuals and as children of God.

Night

*Indeed, the very hairs of your head are all num-
bered. Don't be afraid; you are worth more than
many sparrows.*

LUKE 12:7

When darkness falls and strange shadows take on
a life of their own against the walls of my daughter's
bedroom, she pulls up the covers and waits impatiently
for sleep to protect her from her imagination. This is
only the beginning of how fear will exist in her life.
I pray she discovers the comfort of Your care as new
fears pop up and take shape.

May she feel the blessing of being Your child and
being wanted, known, and protected by the Lord of
all creation. And for every one of those shadows that
emerges, may she have a promise from Your Word
to hold tightly. Whenever darkness returns, may she
ponder Your promises and be confident in her worth
as Your daughter.

Unwrapping Uniqueness

But each man has his own gift from God;
one has this gift, another has that.

1 CORINTHIANS 7:7

My daughter has many layers. I witness many gifts
and talents that You have woven into the fabric of her
being. I see delight in her eyes when she figures out
what makes her unique. But I also see worry cross her
face when she realizes she is different from a friend or
someone she admires.

Help me encourage my daughter. I want to build
her up as she makes more discoveries about her
uniqueness. When I am tempted to shape her in my
image, redirect my motivation. Give me the courage
to raise her up in Your image so that she is able to
celebrate the special person she is.

A Personal Prayer
for My Daughter

Strength

She Wears It Well

She is clothed with strength and dignity;
she can laugh at the days to come.

PROVERBS 31:25

Becoming women isn't easy for girls—learning to speak with conviction and confidence. What do I need to teach my daughter, Lord? How can I give her the gifts of dignity, pride, and also humility? Before me, a girl is unfolding into a woman, and I don't want to miss the opportunity to nurture her journey.

You created my daughter to have strengths seen and unseen. Guide me to recognize these and to help her develop those strengths for good purposes. Clothe her with wisdom so she will seek Your guidance as a girl and as the woman she will become someday.

Never Alone

Be strong and courageous. Do not be afraid or ter-rified because of them, for the LORD your God goes with you; he will never leave you nor forsake you.

DEUTERONOMY 31:6

Children can feel alone in the world as they figure out their way. But they can find strength in numbers, and my daughter never really will stand alone. Help her to feel the love of her parents and of her God as she moves through difficulties, accomplishments, and the times in between. May fears be temporary and never take up residence in her heart.

I know I cannot always be with her physically, but I know You will be with her all the days of her life. Cover her with the peace and strength of Your presence.

Spirited Youth

*Don't let anyone look down on you because you
are young, but set an example for the believers in
speech, in life, in love, in faith and in purity.*

1 TIMOTHY 4:12

The youth have an advantage over the rest of us—
without knowing it or naming it, they savor life's every
moment. They deeply express the joy and the pain
that we so readily cover with experience, maturity, and
reason.

Give my daughter an understanding of how important her contribution is to the betterment of everyone
she meets. Allow her the insight to speak of goodness and to practice a disciplined and giving life. Lord,
open our eyes to the lessons we can learn from the
spirited youth. Prepare me to learn directly from my
daughter.

A Personal Prayer
for My Daughter

Confidence

Never Fear

So we say with confidence, "The Lord is my helper; I will not be afraid. What can man do to me?"

HEBREWS 13:6

Kids like to dress up and pretend to be superheroes. They are invincible as they careen around corners and leap large pillows. Their might is undeniable as they save whoever needs saving. While I watch my daughter playing, a part of me understands that we all have this supernatural help when we trust You with our lives.

Lord, I trust You and entrust my daughter's future to Your care. Today she wears her Sunday school tights and an apron as her cape, and she pretends. I pray that in the years ahead she remains just as fearless. May she soar with confidence that comes from a very real faith and hope in Your help and grace.

A Child's Prayers

This is the confidence we have in approaching
God: that if we ask anything according to his will,
he hears us.

1 JOHN 5:14

I have noticed how my daughter's bedtime prayers have become specific, detailed, and bold over the years. She is learning to trust You with more of her life. She doesn't just bring a wish list anymore. She shares about her friends, her day, her hopes, and her worries. Her prayer time is such a blessing, Lord. I can only imagine how sweet her words are to Your ears.

My heart overflows when I see my child come before her God with confidence and speak to Him with such belief. What a lesson she teaches each evening. Help me to pray more often like a child, Lord.

Something Borrowed

A wife of noble character who can find?
She is worth far more than rubies.
Her husband has full confidence in her
and lacks nothing of value.

PROVERBS 31:10-11

When the day comes for my daughter to walk down the aisle, I pray that her godly character will be as evident as her beauty. And as the man who will be her husband stands with her, may he cherish her as a woman of God and as a strong and loving partner. Lord, lead my daughter to a man who knows You and who sees her value.

That day will hold many splendid memories. The ceremony will start and pass too quickly. But I trust that I will be fully aware of how much my daughter's heart resembles Your own.

A Personal Prayer
for My Daughter

Happiness

Easy Going

*I have learned the secret of being content in any
and every situation, whether well fed or hungry,
whether living in plenty or in want. I can do
everything through him who gives me strength.*

PHILIPPIANS 4:12-13

Our family experienced some tension recently,
God. I could not see eye to eye with my daughter. We
talked over one another, and we said things we didn't
mean. Now I long for peace to return, for us to laugh,
to nudge each other and say we are sorry. It won't take
much. She will make a joke, or I will knock on her
door with an apology.

Knowing it will all be okay is a gift You have given
me. I had to learn this. You showed me how to stop
worrying about every little bump in the road. Our joy
in You will turn our silence and our differences back to
loving conversation and connection once again.

Growing Up

But may the righteous be glad
and rejoice before God;
may they be happy and joyful.

PSALM 68:3

∾

The art of growing up involves a bit of holiness. We are amazed at the maturity our daughter shows. Not always, as You know, but more than a little. She can be graceful and full of grace. Her eyes narrow with sadness when others are in pain. And she draws deep joy from her life experiences.

God, she understands how happiness and gladness are part of the sacred. She draws this out of me when I want to be too serious, too responsible, too prideful. What a blessing my daughter is, Lord. She is helping me grow up—rejoicing and praising all the way.

Let Us Sing

Is anyone happy? Let him sing songs of praise.

JAMES 5:13

∽

We need to celebrate our happiness as a family more often, Lord. I want us to lift up our voices with loud laughter, boisterous talk, and adoring praise. That children's song, "If You're Happy and You Know It," makes me smile. How often do I share a special moment with my daughter and not fully recognize it?

Help me to become satiated with the wonder that surrounds me. Give us a joyful spirit as a family so that our love for You is infectious to those around us. I am happy, and I know it. I will clap my hands in praise today.

A Personal Prayer
for My Daughter

Faith

Jesus Sees

*Jesus turned and saw her. "Take heart, daughter,"
he said, "your faith has healed you." And the
woman was healed from that moment.*

MATTHEW 9:22

My daughter used to think I could fix any hurt
she brought to me. But as she gets older, she understands that many wounds take more than a kiss and a
bandage to make all better. She has hurts, doubts, and
scars that she needs to bring before You. Lord, how
precious is her faith to do just that.

Thank You for being the one who sees my daughter's faith when she looks for healing, for answers,
for someone to listen. You recognize her hurts, even
the ones deep inside her heart and soul. You feel her
hand reaching for You, and You are quick to call her
"daughter."

No Mistakes

The works of his hands are faithful and just;
all his precepts are trustworthy.

PSALM 111:7

The work of Your hands is exquisite, perfect, and detailed. You bring life into being, and You offer life to those willing to receive it. When You formed my daughter, You were faithful. Your promises are a part of her life. And when she stumbles in her belief, the longing she has for You soon eases her mind and spirit and clears her path. You point out the way for her to walk forward, trusting You to be there.

I will make mistakes—as will my daughter. But You do not make mistakes. The heart You have placed in my child beats with a longing to know her Maker better.

Reflecting You

*Love the L*ORD *your God with all your heart and with all your soul and with all your strength. These commandments that I give you today are to be upon your hearts. Impress them on your children. Talk about them when you sit at home and when you walk along the road, when you lie down and when you get up.*

DEUTERONOMY 6:5-7

My daughter makes talking of Your unconditional love easy for me. Just the fact that she is in my life seems proof of Your faithfulness. When we notice the change of seasons, her eyes get wide with wonder. She sees Your miracles for what they are—gifts. Bedtime, mealtimes, and moments of praise bring our hearts together in prayer, and she witnesses our dependence on You as Provider and Giver.

Shape my actions, words, and motivations to be pleasing to You, Lord. I long to reflect my heavenly Parent's love and nurture my daughter's faith even in the most normal, everyday moments.

A Personal Prayer for My Daughter

Security

Faithful Forever

Your faithfulness continues through all genera-
tions; you established the earth, and it endures.

PSALM 119:90

I place so much emphasis on time. Deadlines,
appointments, birthdays, playdates. Time passes, seasons change, a fresh new calendar kicks off a new year,
and we start the process again. But Lord, You are not
limited by schedules, by time. Your faithfulness does
not expire but continues, flourishes, and covers us.

Thank You for being the God of forever for my
daughter, my family, and for future generations. Our
details come and go, but Your plans and purposes
remain.

Love Perseveres

*Love does not delight in evil but rejoices with the
truth. It always protects, always trusts, always
hopes, always perseveres.*

1 CORINTHIANS 13:6-7

I am sad sometimes to see my daughter growing
up so quickly. Yet I know she will be an adult in no
time. My prayer today is about her future security. I
pray for her heart to be protected, not from ever being
hurt, but from breaking in a way that breaks her faith
and spirit.

Lord, if I can ask such things, my hope is that true
love will be a part of her life. I want her to know what
it means to trust love's goodness, faithfulness, and
future. And if hurt does happen along the way, help
her hold out for the love and security You have waiting
for her.

There Is Hope

You will be secure, because there is hope;
you will look about you and take your rest
in safety.

JOB 11:18

We don't need much more than hope. We think we do, but we don't. Lord, Your gifts of security and stability are the radiance of hope, shining brightly in our lives even when we face our darkest hours. We can move forward with assurance because You are there to guide us through the storm.

God, shine Your hope into my daughter's life and along her path. When the clouds roll in and the sea of change and disappointment begins to sway beneath her feet, let her turn to You. Give her rest and renewal in the safety of Your promises.

A Personal Prayer
for My Daughter

Whimsy

Silly Times

Let them praise his name with dancing
and make music to him with tambourine
and harp.

PSALM 149:3

My daughter likes to dress up, play make-believe, build forts, and braid her hair in funny styles. When I sense one of us is stressed, I turn up the music, and we dance. Soon we are calling out what we each are thankful for. How simply we can reach for the joy in our day, Lord. We need only to sing, make music, and praise Your name, and our mood, our spirits, and our outlook are transformed.

Help me see that whether we have cause for celebration or a mood change, we always have a reason to sing and praise Your name—we are Your daughters. Let us rejoice.

Full of Surprises

*Sarah said, "God has brought me laughter,
and everyone who hears about this will laugh
with me."*

GENESIS 21:6

My daughter is full of surprises. Her smile. Her kindness. The clever remarks and thoughtful comments that she offers up at dinner or in the car on the way to the store. People comment that she is her own person. But I know that she is Yours completely.

As my daughter seeks independence from me, she worries what I will say, what I will do to embarrass her. Sometimes I have the same worries about her. But the flip side of worry is surprise—and we both delight one another, and I pray we delight You as we both make our way as independent women of faith.

Party

*They will celebrate your abundant goodness
and joyfully sing of your righteousness.*

PSALM 145:7

Set in my daughter a fantastic spark, an unquench-able desire for the divine. Fill her with all the wonders of Your beauty and wisdom. When she gets caught up in the daily grind of responsibilities and concerns that Your creation is prone to obsess over, jolt her with joy.

I want her life to be full, overflowing with the blessing You offer. We need to learn to reach for it, grab it, pray for it, look for it, and cherish it. As a parent, I'm inclined to focus on lessons about duty, follow-through, and responsible citizenship. Don't let me forget to teach her how to rejoice, celebrate, and sing of Your righteousness.

A Personal Prayer for My Daughter

Righteousness

Open Faith

I do not hide your righteousness in my heart;
I speak of your faithfulness and salvation.
I do not conceal your love and your truth
from the great assembly.

PSALM 40:10

Am I too silent about my faith, Lord? Does my life encourage my daughter to be open about her beliefs? I want to create an environment in our home that inspires others. Let us be a family that comforts those in need and opens our doors to those wanting to belong.

When I feel the urging of the Spirit to talk to others about matters of faith, give me the courage and willingness to obey. May I lead by example so that my daughter never feels ashamed by her faith, but only blessed to share it.

A Humble Spirit

Good and upright is the LORD;
therefore he instructs sinners in his ways.
He guides the humble in what is right
and teaches them his way.

PSALM 25:8-9

My pride as a parent can get in the way of my daughter's humility. When I am beaming about one of her successes or moments of personal victory, I have gloated a time or two. God of goodness and uprightness, help me always give You credit while congratulating and supporting my daughter so that she associates You with all of her blessings.

Let us be mindful and prayerful of Your hand on our lives so that we give You the credit and learn the lessons of humility, contentment, and fairness. When we suffer loss, make mistakes, and experience moments we would rather forget, let us be gracious. And let us thank You for those lessons too.

Wanting to Be Right

Stop doing wrong,
learn to do right!
Seek justice,
encourage the oppressed.

ISAIAH 1:16-17

Last night we heard hollering in our home along with the sound of a door slamming several times. My daughter is not happy about something. It is not something life threatening or even life changing, though I can see in her eyes that she believes it to be both. I tend to feel like an oppressed victim when her anger boils over, but I can see she is wounded by the circumstance.

Help me encourage her toward a right attitude without fueling her frustration. Guide me to choose words that breathe peace into the situation so that she can learn how to do right even when she is hurt.

A Personal Prayer for My Daughter

Prayer

Turning to God

*Surely then you will find delight in the Almighty
and will lift up your face to God.
You will pray to him, and he will hear you,
and you will fulfill your vows.*

JOB 22:26-27

"Look at me when I am talking to you." I used to say this when my daughter was little. She would stare out the window when I was trying to teach her to count, read, or eat. Now I hope that she turns her face and her attention to You, Lord. When You are teaching her something important, may she listen with intention and then speak from her heart.

I pray she turns to look at You for guidance and love and even to learn lessons that don't seem as interesting as the nearest distraction.

Passionate Prayer

Shout with joy to God, all the earth!
Sing the glory of his name;
make his praise glorious!
Say to God, "How awesome are your deeds!"

PSALM 66:1-3

She exudes excitement. My daughter can barely contain herself when she is happy. Oh, how I hope she never loses this childlike passion. As she grows older, I pray she brings You the pleasure of her delight. Her wide eyes will turn to You with expectation and anticipation. I can see her tapping her toes and clapping her hands in Your presence—eager to share her day and her dreams with You.

How awesome is Your name, Lord. You hear a young girl's prayers, and You take joy in her passionate heart, which seeks You and sings Your praises.

Should the Day Come

I will give them a heart to know me, that I am the LORD. They will be my people, and I will be their God, for they will return to me with all their heart.

JEREMIAH 24:7

You have a hold on my daughter's heart. I see it in the way she speaks of You in her precious, young faith. Her evening prayers are simple and sincere. Often she asks what You would want us to do when we have a family decision to make.

But Lord, should the day come when she steps away from the path of faith, let my prayer now be saved, held, and heard—allow her knowledge of You in these years to lead her back to You. I pray her heart always brings her back to her Father.

A Personal Prayer
for My Daughter

Heart

Servanthood

*Whatever you do, work at it with all your heart,
as working for the Lord, not for men, since you
know that you will receive an inheritance from
the Lord as a reward. It is the Lord Christ you are
serving.*

COLOSSIANS 3:23-24

My daughter's life will seem to have many masters—schoolwork and teachers, jobs and bosses. Her efforts might be divided by many loyalties. Give her a heart that is steadfast in the priorities You have for her. Grant her a spirit of discernment so that she can follow Your leading.

Let her quest and reward be a servant's giving spirit. May she see through the earthly masters and keep her eyes and heart on her heavenly Master, Teacher, and Lord.

Take It to Heart

Acknowledge and take to heart this day that the
LORD is God in heaven above and on the earth
below. There is no other.

DEUTERONOMY 4:39

What sinks into the depths of my daughter's heart?
Is she gleaning the lessons about faith and love that
we are trying to teach her? Does she know You well?
I pray her heart calls on You throughout the day. Her
life is pretty protected—we work to keep her safe
and healthy. But Lord, I know she will have times of
struggle and disappointment. Seasons will come when
I am not the person she turns to when she faces dif-
ficulty or loneliness.

I pray she takes her relationship with You to heart
and holds it tight because there is no other God in
heaven or on earth.

Without a Doubt

You know with all your heart and soul that not one of all the good promises the LORD your God gave you has failed.

JOSHUA 23:14

Trends and fascinations capture my daughter's attention and interest. But that interest fades. The "in crowd's" acceptance or rejection keeps her guessing and worried. On top of that, she has to discover that her parents are human and fallible. Lord, keep her heart and soul grounded in Your unconditional and infallible promises.

May every fiber of her being know the certainty of Your unfailing love. When other people and situations let her down, give her the strength and character to depend on her Provider. Please, Lord—let her cling to this truth.

A Personal Prayer
for My Daughter

Integrity

Worthwhile

Always give yourselves fully to the work of the Lord, because you know that your labor in the Lord is not in vain.

1 CORINTHIANS 15:58

I am not sure what to do when my daughter wants to give up on something or someone. An on-demand culture practically shouts, "Throw it away, move on," if a problem requires solving or a project demands time and patience. My child's life is already torn in many directions, so at the first sign of labor she is looking for an out.

Instill in me the wisdom to direct her onward and forward in all that she does. Help me show her that fully investing oneself is a way to honor You. And to be a good example, may I also honor the importance of a job well done.

Package Deal

Guard my life and rescue me;
let me not be put to shame,
for I take refuge in you.
May integrity and uprightness protect me,
because my hope is in you.

PSALM 25:20-21

Guard my daughter's heart from the spiritual ailments of her generation—apathy, pride, discontentment, and hopelessness. I pray she seeks Your aid when any of these characteristics enter her life. How happy we will be to see her stand upright and with integrity as a young woman and in later years.

Pave the way for my daughter to discover whom the Protector of her soul and spirit truly is. Let the brilliance of Your everlasting hope lead her to Your refuge.

Fear and Fortitude

Charm is deceptive, and beauty is fleeting;
but a woman who fears the LORD is to be praised.

PROVERBS 31:30

Occasionally I strike a bit of fear in my daughter. Usually the moment involves guessing she is sneaking cookies a couple rooms away. But this does not breed respect; it just makes her more careful. Lord, how can I help my daughter have a healthy fear of You? I know it will lead to strength, character, and integrity.

I want to plant the seeds of this fear in my daughter's heart so she will grow into a woman who loves her Lord and who respects His will and His purpose for her. May she never view You as the one who will catch her at things, but rather as the one who will keep her in His care.

A Personal Prayer for My Daughter

Contentment

Compare and Contrast

*I know what it is to be in need, and I know what
it is to have plenty. I have learned the secret of
being content in any and every situation, whether
well fed or hungry, whether living in plenty or in
want. I can do everything through him who gives
me strength.*

PHILIPPIANS 4:12-13

Lord, our household needs a perspective shift. My
daughter returned from a friend's grand birthday party
and promptly was disappointed with her room, her
belongings, and the plans for her upcoming party. We
all can occasionally determine our happiness by com-
paring our situation with our neighbor, a friend, or
someone we hear about on television.

Give us the godly measure for our contentment.
Help us praise You for another day as Your children
and for this chance to be in fellowship with our Creator. No comparison necessary—it's all good.

Money Talk

*Keep your lives free from the love of money and be
content with what you have, because God has said,
"Never will I leave you; never will I forsake you."*

HEBREWS 13:5

My daughter has a keen eye for money. She sees it
and grabs it. Already she assumes it has an important
role to play in happiness. God, we try not to empha-
size the importance of money except for the power of
giving and how it helps us live and serve You—but I
see it will take effort to separate money from contentment.

I pray that the true priorities and blessings will rise
up in my daughter's life. Help us redirect her attention
to the only source of joy and worth—Your grace.

Untouchables

The fear of the LORD leads to life:
Then one rests content, untouched by trouble.

PROVERBS 19:23

I am learning from my daughter how to laugh it off. Her youthful innocence helps me through moments when I would rather take the bumpy road of regret or anger. Can You preserve that spirit in her, Lord? Is there a way to protect her vibrant joy so that she does not become jaded by the trappings of adulthood?

Deep in my soul, my biggest prayer is for this lovely creature's heart to remain untouched by the disappointment misguided priorities can cause. But I should not worry—she is learning to trust You and to happily accept each day's offerings.

A Personal Prayer for My Daughter

Wholeness

Full Circle

*God is love. Whoever lives in love lives in God,
and God in him. In this way, love is made complete among us so that we will have confidence on
the day of judgment, because in this world we are
like him.*

1 JOHN 4:16-17

We were gazing at the night sky when a sense of
wholeness came over us. We are living within Your
creation. We lift up our praises and prayers to You,
and still we are a part of You and You are a part of us.
Your love flows through me, my daughter, our family,
the strangers we pass on the street. Love is our connection.

My daughter might not remember that night sky,
but may she always stare into Your eyes with amazement and adoration. Your love in her will bring wholeness, healing, and salvation.

No Halfway

Be diligent in these matters; give yourself wholly to them, so that everyone may see your progress.

1 TIMOTHY 4:15

You plant faith lessons in many different situations—even in my daughter's homework. She was doing it in a rather fast and messy way. We had a conversation about how doing something halfheartedly is not really finishing it. God, what if You had rushed through the part about forming man and woman, or the seas, the animals?

You must be disappointed when Your creation does things without diligence and thoughtfulness. Homework might not be shaping the world, but it is shaping my daughter's mind and future. I pray we can teach her to do things well, wholly, and with pride.

Asking for Help

"Lord, I want to see," he replied. Jesus said to him,
"Receive your sight; your faith has healed you."
Immediately he received his sight and followed
Jesus, praising God. When all the people saw it,
they also praised God.

LUKE 18:41-42

Shyness can keep my daughter from verbalizing what she needs. Behind strands of hair, if she builds up her courage, she will quietly ask for a glass of water, a Band-Aid, a place to rest. I don't want my child to be afraid of speaking her mind or her heart, especially when she comes to You. Let her words be loud and clear and filled with sincerity when she brings her future battles, wounds, and brokenness to Your attention.

I will praise You today for giving my daughter the chance to come before her Father boldly with her needs—knowing she will be heard.

A Personal Prayer
for My Daughter

Voice

Who, Me?

But Moses said to the LORD, "Since I speak with faltering lips, why would Pharaoh listen to me?"

EXODUS 6:30

I know my child will discover her strengths and step forward with conviction when she faces an important task. Right now, she tends to waiver, wait, and then worry after she has missed her opportunity. Lord, how do I build up her confidence? How do we let her know that what she has to say is important, what she has to offer is significant?

Those around my daughter see her potential, but until she places her trust in You, I know she will not have a say in her success. She will hide behind past mistakes and insecurities. I see myself in her when she is afraid. Lord, help her feel Your calling in her life so that she can reach for her dreams and speak of Your goodness.

Speaking Up

*But I desire to speak to the Almighty and to argue
my case with God.*

JOB 13:3

We tell girls not to raise their voices. But Lord,
sometimes I want my daughter to use strong, clear
words. I want her to give life and volume to her opin-
ions and ideas. I pray she is able to articulate her faith
with words that inspire.

When she faces the mountains and valleys in her
journey, my hope is that she will call out to You with
raw emotion. Hushed tones that do not disturb the
calm are sometimes appropriate. But at other times, a
girl, a woman needs to shout, cry, and raise her voice.
May You hear her and be proud.

Make It Count

But Joshua had commanded the people, "Do not give a war cry, do not raise your voices, do not say a word until the day I tell you to shout. Then shout!"

JOSHUA 6:10

Kids can talk incessantly for hours and not seem to have any point. This chatter has become the soundtrack to my days. I try to participate and encourage, but I find myself wanting my daughter to slow her thoughts down. To make them count.

Eventually, she will be more careful expressing her emotions. So help me encourage my daughter to talk, to explore her imagination and ideas, to discuss her favorite books, flowers, and colors. The string of words she laces from room to room are full of wonder. I need to make them count. These beautiful words tear down walls between us.

A Personal Prayer for My Daughter

Work

Praise at the Gates

Give her the reward she has earned,
and let her works bring her praise at the city gate.

PROVERBS 31:31

My daughter's city gate is the front porch, where she sells lemonade to passersby, lured by warm weather, fair prices, and a cute smile. When patrons compliment her business savvy and her customer service, she beams.

I pray, Lord, that my daughter finds satisfaction and reward all of her working life, in whatever endeavors she puts her hands to. May she always deal honestly with people and use the fruits of her work wisely. Let her labors, large and small, honor You.

Time-Outs: The Good Kind

By the seventh day God had finished the work he had been doing; so on the seventh day he rested from all his work.

GENESIS 2:2

Father God, my daughter certainly understands the difference between work and play. But rest? Not so much.

Help us both discern when we need to refrain from busyness. In this world of playdates and Day-Timers, help my daughter recognize the value of downtime. As You sought rest from the creation of the world, as Christ sought quiet and prayer in the full days of His ministry, may she too find renewal in stillness.

Blessings Always at Hand

The LORD your God has blessed you in all the
work of your hands. He has watched over your
journey through this vast desert.

DEUTERONOMY 2:7

My daughter looks up to older children. She admires the quality of their artwork, their ability at games, their shouldering of increased responsibility. I pray that even at this young age, she will see the blessing in all the works of her own hands.

May she suspend her own and others' judgment and see instead Your hand on her life journey, Your pacing of her milestones, and your guidance and affirmation in times tough and joyful.

A Personal Prayer for My Daughter

Patience

Seeing It Through

*Consider it pure joy, my brothers, whenever you
face trials of many kinds, because you know that
the testing of your faith develops perseverance.
Perseverance must finish its work so that you may
be mature and complete, not lacking anything.*

JAMES 1:2-4

Stubbornness and perseverance have a lot in
common, but the fruits they bear are so different.
Help my daughter see the difference between digging
in when troubles come and digging deep to find Your
abundant grace.

The act of perseverance is something we cannot do
rightly without You. We depend on Your strength to
carry on. Show my daughter that joy is to be found in
the process as well as in the prize.

Peace, Sister

Be completely humble and gentle; be patient,
bearing with one another in love. Make every
effort to keep the unity of the Spirit through the
bond of peace.

EPHESIANS 4:2-3

I really like that "Make every effort" part, Lord. It
sounds like a parent. It sounds like me exhorting my
daughter to "try your very best" when she encounters
a rough patch in a relationship.

We are so tempted, in our humanness, to barrel
through a challenge rather than to bear with a brother
or sister or friend. Let my daughter become that rare,
rare thing—a humble, gentle, and patient soul. May
she always seek unity over division and achieve it
through love—Your love.

Won't You Come In?

Be joyful in hope, patient in affliction, faithful in prayer. Share with God's people who are in need. Practice hospitality.

ROMANS 12:12-13

As my daughter sits among her playthings, creating worlds for her animals, dolls, and friends, I find myself listening in. Is she being kind? Patient? Fair? Every day I'm getting glimpses of the woman she will be all too soon.

I pray, Lord, that You will prompt her with Your Spirit and that she will attune herself to You. May hope, patience, faithfulness, prayerfulness, and hospitality be more than adornments brought out at special times. Make these qualities sincere parts of who she is so that others see You in her attitudes and actions.

A Personal Prayer
for My Daughter

Purity

Keep Her

To the pure, all things are pure, but to those who are corrupted and do not believe, nothing is pure.

TITUS 1:15

This girl I love so much—keep her in Your arms. Rock her slowly when her soul weeps. With acceptance and patience, welcome her to sit on Your lap. Tenderly stroke her hair when she is afraid. Teach her Your will for her life.

Lord, preserve her innocence and guard her heart from corruption and disbelief. I see how accepting she is of life, of people, and I am moved by her purity. She is evidence of Your pure compassion and mercy.

Reflections

To the faithful you show yourself faithful,
to the blameless you show yourself blameless,
to the pure you show yourself pure,
but to the crooked you show yourself shrewd.

2 SAMUEL 22:26-27

Games are for the young and old. As I find myself in-between, I am less inclined to play. My daughter giggles and invests herself in fun with fabulous energy. *You get out what you put into something.* I arise with half of my daughter's zest for adventure and openness. Her clean slate welcomes whatever You will scribe for her day.

May You always be the force of faithfulness and purity in my daughter's life. As for me, my heart is being polished and renewed. I pray for faith like my daughter's and for a soul that reflects and gives less of me and more of You.

What God Looks Like

Blessed are the pure in heart, for they will see God.

MATTHEW 5:8

～

Looking at life and the world through my daughter's eyes has given me a perspective of joy. My tendencies toward worry and responsibility have altered my view of wonder and delight. To step from my outlook and to see everything afresh is good for me.

Your miracles abound in my daily life. My daughter is quick to notice, and I am learning. She is teaching me how to look at You with reverence and excitement. Even my faith had become routine and mundane. Now I ask my daughter, in all her wholesomeness and honesty, to describe You. She sees You and You see her. And I keep learning.

She Is Yours

*Now I commit you to God and to the word of his
grace, which can build you up and give you an
inheritance among all those who are sanctified.*

ACTS 20:32

It is what needs to be done, this letting go of my
daughter slowly and surely. I want to hold her hand
forever and clear the way on her behalf. I never felt
this desire to hold on before my daughter entered my
life and my care. You are her original and eternal Care-
taker. I believe this completely yet rely on Your grace
to truly trust it.

I commit her to You and to the journey You shape
for her. Yes, she is a part of my lineage, but she is a
stepping-stone in Your legacy of faith. I let go because
I must—I am able to because You will hold her hand
and heart forever and make her way.